Incidents Connected with the Life of Selim Aga

I0447418

Incidents Connected with the Life of Selim Aga, A Native of Central Africa:
By

Aga Selim

Incidents Connected with the Life of Selim Aga

DEDICATION.

TO MRS. THURBURN.

MURTLE, *June*, 1846.

MADAM,--Having written a short account of some incidents connected with my life, I return my grateful and sincere thanks to you for the great interest you have taken in my education, by which means I have been brought from African darkness to a knowledge of the comforts of a civilized and social life. Hitherto, for these ten years, I have experienced your benevolent care and tuition, and have been elevated far above many of my poor countrymen, whose minds are lying with the dust. To whom should I ascribe this work, if not to the patroness of my education? To whom should I dedicate these incidents, if not to the guardian of my younger years? Yes, Madam; to you, and to you alone, I now acknowledge my gratitude for the many benefits which I enjoy. Although far distant from kindred and relations--although far from the care of an overlooking mother--I have found in you, Madam, a truly good substitute for these wants. I have experienced your goodness in sending me to school, and putting me in the hands of one whose whole interest was absorbed in teaching the young idea how to shoot. In whatever circumstanees my lot may be cast, I hope your private admonitions will render me impregnable when attacked by the many vices prevalent in the world.

I have the honour to be,
MADAM,
Your most obedt. Servant,

SELIM AGA.

CONTENTS.

Incidents Connected with the Life of Selim Aga

PREFACE

IT is not the Author's intention to make great orations out of nothing, nor to picture the description of his country in eloquent language, but to give, in the form of recollections, a brief account of incidents connected with his own life. Having been urged by several friends to write an account of his life, he hopes that this small work will meet the approbation of all who read it. He will not fail, therefore, to make it as interesting as possible. The reader, however, must not expect something extraordinary when beginning to read this narrative. Great anxiety has been felt by geographical and other societies, to obtain an accurate knowledge of Africa and its products. Of these, the Author is sorry that he cannot satisfy his readers, having been taken away from his country at a very early age. Of all the quarters of the globe, Africa is the least known. Ignorance, barbarity, and superstition, prevail in its centre, and the unhealthy nature of its climate renders it almost impracticable for any European to travel into it, and satisfy an enquiring public. Taking a natural view of the country, it is barren, sandy, and mountainous, interspersed with a few green spots, called oases, or made fertile by the inundation of some river in the rainy season. Taking an artificial view of those regions, you will perceive nothing but a few small huts here and there, built by the inhabitants for their own accommodation. The Northern and Southern States can boast of a little civilization, being frequented and inhabited by the dwellers of the north temperate zone. In taking a political view of the centre of Africa, the enquirer will find the country divided into a number of small principalities, who maintain their dignity by making war against each other. The captives taken in these wars are sold as slaves, being purchased by Arabs and Turks on the east coast, and Spaniards, Portuguese, and Americans, on the west. Thus many of these poor creatures are brought to a level with the brute beasts, by the inhabitants of that federal government, (the United States), who pretend to profess the principles of freedom and Christianity in their truest light. The selling of these captives stimulates others to kidnap some of the poor natives, and carry on a brutal traffic in buying and selling human victims for the gratification of their own ambitious propensities. In this manner the fate of the author was sealed. The author will proceed to detail the events of his history in the form of recollections.

SELIM AGA.

AGA'S RECOLLECTIONS.

DESCRIPTION OF THE VALLEY OF TEGLA, AND ITS INHABITANTS.

SURROUNDED by some beautiful mountain scenery, and situated between Durfur and Abyssinia, is a small valley going under the denomination of Tegla, or Tegeley. To this valley I stretch forth my affections, giving it the endearing appellation of my native home and father land. It was there that I was born; 'twas there that I received the fond looks of a loving mother; and it was there that I set my feet for the first time upon a world full of cares, trials, difficulties, and dangers. I cannot give the exact limits of the valley of Tegla. There were, however, three Chiefs who exercised power over its inhabitants. Mehemet Chammaroo (under whose government my father was) ruled the centre; while two other princes had the sway, one on each side. Like many of the regions bordering on the equator, the valley of Tegla is exposed to the excessive heat of the burning sun. Its seasons, properly speaking, can only be divided into two parts--the rainy and the dry season. In the rainy season agriculture is carried on by the farmer on a very small scale--the only substitute for a plough being a long pole, with something similar to a shovel attached to the end of it. With this instrument the surface of the ground is broken, after which the seed (consisting of Indian corn and maize) is sown in small quantities at certain distances from each other. After it has grown a certain length, part of it is transplanted into different fields, thus giving the crop full scope and encouragement to grow. When the corn begins to change colour, the rainy season declines, till at length the refulgent rays of the sun perceive the inhabitant of the vale preparing to reap his harvest. The rain is over, the dry season is on; many begin to reap the fruits of their labour.

> * *How wisely has Providence ordered all things. The inhabitants of Egypt have no rain, and yet the river Nile has its yearly inundations. The rainy season in the valley of Tegla, and its neighbouring countries forms tributaries to the Nile; makes it overflow its banks; spreads fertility through the muddy soil of the country; and supplies its dependant natives with the necessaries of life.*

My juvenile recollections did not bring the nature of the implements used for shearing. The shearers are not formed of a number of mercenaries, who expect to pocket shillings and half-crowns at the end of their period of labour; but such is the social nature of the people among themselves, that they exchange services with each other. A large concourse of them assemble in the harvest field; and, in a very short time, the harvest is taken in. The day of shearing is generally ended with dancing, of which amusement they are very fond. The reader, perhaps, will inquire what sort of drink these dancers use? His mind will very likely answer, Jamaica rum, French brandy, or Irish whisky. But no; water is their chief drink. They have a thick intoxicating liquor, which they make from the

Indian corn; but such a luxury is only used on extraordinary occasions. After all their harvest festivities are over, they give themselves up to all the indolent habits prevalent in these eastern countries; and lounge in their booths until the appearance of the skies proclaim the distant approach of the rainy season.

Widely different is the dry season, when compared with the rainy. In the dry season the inhabitant of the vale employs his time with various pursuits; in the rainy, nothing but agriculture occupies his attention. In the dry season he has to dig wells to supply his household with water; in the rainy, he has only to go to the rivulets for that supply. The dry season carries off all traces of water; scorches all the grass and green trees; occasions deep chasms in the earth; and leaves the poor native nothing to depend upon but his industry in the rainy season. Indian corn, maize, and a flock of goats are generally all his treasure. Money is not valued. The valley of Tegla boasts of no cows, although many are kept in its vicinity. Prince Chammaroo's dominions had only three wells. The different districts regularly awaited their turn in receiving a supply of water. The religion is Paganism, mixed with several Mahommedan rites, such as the shaving of their heads, circumcision, and fasting; but their chief attention is attracted to the sun, the moon, and stars.

* Building, hunting, travelling, and warfare, generally in this season. Every grown up man is a warrior.

About a month after the ceremony of circumcision, a number of young men convene at the house where the rite had been performed, and sally from thence through the country on hunting excursions. Everything falls a prey to the hunter's knife and spear; and on these occasions the poultry-yard suffers most, while the poor owners are mere lookers on at these depredations, it being deemed sacred to interfere with the behaviour of these young men. Fasting is also very strictly observed by the devotee, one month in the year being alloted for that purpose. Before daybreak, he rises and eats, and never again tastes anything, until the evening stars declare the shades of night, when he breaks his fast and retires to rest. The houses in the valley of Tegla are built in a style peculiar to themselves. Every room is built about ten or twenty yards from eaeh other, of a round form, with thatch roofs. The under part of the rooms are built of stones and mud; the roofs are thatched with the maize and Indian corn canes. Four or five rooms form a respectable dwelling, the whole of which are enclosed by a wall about five feet high, thus leaving an open square in the centre. In the great heat of the dry season, this square is used by the indwellers for sleeping apartments, where they all lie down on the floor, and cover themselves with a large white sheet. If disturbed by any wild beasts during the night, they betake themselves to the inner rooms. My father's house consisted of two bedrooms, a kitchen, a mill room, and a goat room, or fold. Goats' milk is considered a very wholesome commodity; it has a pleasing sweet taste, which attracts the palate to it, and is said to possess a certain virtue in medicinal qualities. The junior male members of the family are employed in taking care of the flock. When a number of them are going in the same direction they mix their flocks together, and each in his turn mutually takes care of the whole flock till evening, when, by a cry peculiar to each goat-herd, his flock separates from the rest, and follows him. He then takes them home, gets them milked, and secures them in the fold. Those which are great favourites are generally taken into the sleeping apartments. The milk must not be allowed to stand till the middle of next day, else it would get quite sour. In order to prevent this catastrophe they either drink it or make butter of it. Their mode of churning is as follows:--

The gourd or calabash, which grows plentifully in these districts, is a plant something similar to a melon plant. It's fruit is like a melon, but the inside is bitter. The gourd melons grow to different sizes, so that the natives make dishes and plates out of them, by cutting them into halves. The churn, however, requires a whole melon, and one of the largest is taken for that purpose. After a part of the pith is taken out, it is filled with water, and permitted to stand till the inside is quite rotten. It is then cleaned out, secured into a rope basket, suspended to the roof of one of the rooms, so as it can be reached by a person standing, and there it serves as a churn,--the dairymaid's work being to put the milk into it, and work it to and fro with her hands. No cream is extracted.

The butter is generally used for rubbing their skins; and very little clothing being used, many of them could be seen standing out in the sun like a number of polished statues. After washing themselves with water, they never think that they are complete till they rub some butter on their skins. The dress among the higher classes is a long wide gown, reaching to the ancles, and wide open sleeves, so as not to confine the wearer too much, and sandals on their feet. The lower classes, again, have a long wide plaid, which they tie round their body, and over one of their shoulders, leaving the other quite free; while in length it only reaches to the knees. This forms all their variety of dress.

Their food is entirely confined to the Indian corn, served up in different ways. They seldom kill their goats for butcher meat, having a great desire to preserve a large stock.

Having given a short account of the customs of my native country, I shall now relate my own history.

SELF-HISTORY.--YOUTH AND PREMATURE SLAVERY.

YOUTH is the period in which true happiness is enjoyed. It is the time when all trials and difficulties seem to lie in oblivion; and it is then that all principles can be instilled into the tender mind. The mind in youth is not prejudiced, builds many castles in the air although without any symptoms of ambition, is pleased and always desires to please. It is like the shoot of a tender flower ere its leaves expand. It is the germ on which strong propensities and sentiments are framed. It is in youth that the stronger faculties of the artist, the genius, and the mechanic are pictured. None of these propensities, however, were predominant in my mind while home was my residence. Being the oldest of the boys, my pride was raised to no small degree when I beheld my father preparing a farm for me. This event filled my mind with the grand anticipation of leaving the goats to my brother, who was then beginning to work a little. While my father was making these preparations, I had the constant charge of the goats; and being accompanied by two other boys who resided near my father's house, we wandered many miles from home, by which means we acquired an acquaintance with the different districts of the country. 'Twas while in these rambles with my companions that I became the victim of the slaveholder. While tending our flock between two hills, we spied two men shaping their course towards us. They inquired whether we had any goats for them, a term quite common in that country. Our reply was, of course, in the negative; but they merely used this craft in order to deprive us of suspicion. Myself being nearest to them, I was firmly secured in their hands, and forced away whether I would or not.

On showing symptoms of resistance, one of them procured a green twig, and whipped me till the blood was falling in drops from my legs. After proceeding some miles, we came to a house, where I was tied with ropes hand and foot, and laid down to rest. Next morning, before dawn of day, my cruel master took the ropes off my legs, and, setting me on a certain direction, desired me to walk while he followed with a large whip. Terrified out of my judgment, I saw that there was nothing to be done but either do or suffer. I of course chose the former. This was rather a harsh treatment for a child of eight years of age. Commencing before sunrise, we continued our journey till the middle of the day, when we arrived at a village. This village went under the name of Tegla. At the village of Tegla my inhuman master disposed of me, and returned home. On entering the house of my new master, what was my astonishment on seeing an old acquaintance there, a girl with whom I had an interview a few weeks previous. She, poor creature, had also fallen into the hands of the enemy only a few days before myself. This girl, whose name was Medina, admonished me on this occasion, telling me to do whatever I was desired, assuring me that the white man would not care for taking our lives, that the killing of us would not cost him a thought.

We were well secured with iron chains on our feet, and were never permitted to go far from the house. We could never fall upon plans for effecting our escape, although we often tried different means for that purpose. One night I managed to get the chains off my feet, and would have escaped had not the fear of being recaptured prevented me. Notwithstanding all the plans which Medina resorted to, she could not get the chains off her feet. A short time after this, a caravan (consisting of merchants and travellers) left the village of Tegla. With this caravan our master joined, and, after a day's journey, we arrived at a small village, where he was disappointed in his object, viz., the disposing of us into another's hands, therefore he had no other recourse but to return to his own country. Arriving at the village, we received the heart-rending intelligence that our friends had been in search of us, and were frustrated, having heard that we were taken to a distant land. Another caravan was soon equipped for a farther distance. This was some four day's journey from the village of Tegla, to a large town called Kordofan, under the jurisdiction of the Pacha of Egypt. The first night we pitched our tents at a well of water, not having seen a single house on the whole of our journey. The second day we continued our journey till late at night, when we received the guidance of some light from a distant village, where we arrived and reposed ourselves. This village was called by the natives Albaharr, or, as seen on our maps, Albeit. The inhabitants are a people who might be distinguished among a thousand different nations. Such is their love of jewellery, that they wear rings on their nostrils as well as ears. Instead of horses, or donkeys, or camels, they ride upon bullocks, the noses of which are also adorned with rings, and to these the bridles are tied. We stayed a few days at this place, and shared the unfeigned hospitality of the people, who were uncommonly kind. During our stay here, Medina and I were taken to the camp of the Turks, not far away from the village, where we were put through different exercises. The first thing we were desired to do was to show our tongues, and then our teeth. The rest of our limbs underwent a serious examination also. Having undergone this examination, we were taken back to our lodgings again. The next day our master joined the Turks, who were returning to Kordofan, and by that means ensured our fate of never returning to our native country. In two days we reached the point of our destination, and there our master disposed of us to an Arab, with whom we lived but two or three days. From an Arab we fell into the hands of a Turk. My time while with the first three masters was employed doing nothing. The Turkish gentleman found work for every body; and all the testimony I can bear to his good character is, that he was one of the cruelest men in existence.

Being an officer of the rank of an aga, his men suffered many harsh cruelties under him. On one occasion, a soldier having been brought to his house for a small offence, he took the office of corporal; and commanding four men to hold him down, beat the poor man, till the blood was running from his cheeks. The keeper of his camels often suffered in a similar way. My office was what might be called a general house-servant. The duties of waiting the table, washing dishes, making coffee, and waiting for orders, were allotted to me as my share of the work. Medina was made assistant cook for a short time, but I had the disagreeable misfortune to see her sold to another Turk; thus I was left to suffer alone.

Some six months, however, relieved me of my hardships. To mention all the cruelties I suffered at that time, would be quite needless. I will only notify a few of them. My master, on whom I had continually to attend, punished every small fault with great severity. If he called, he said I ought to hear him at whatever distance I might be. At one time, being sent from home by my mistress, my master interrogated me on my return with where have you been, and began to thrash me. Self-justification was of no use. No moderate blows did with him, for while he struck one side of my head, he met it at the other side also. I became almost insensible, while the blood was running out of my ears. At another time, having made some coffee by his own orders, I happened to make a few cups more than was required. He said nothing at the time; but after I was in bed, he got hold of a horse whip, and coming upon me unawares, thrashed me till I was quite speechless. I am persuaded he would have killed me had not one of the domestics heard my cries, and come to my rescue. Here I may mention that a very small child can stop a Mahomedan from revenging himself to too great an extent, by taking the whip, or whatever he uses, from him. One of the slaves was the means of preventing my master from whipping me any longer. In Kordofan the houses are all of one storey high. The part in which I lived was chiefly occupied by officers in the Pacha's service. My master was married, had two children, two female slaves, two males, and myself. The other two being grown-up men, were taken out to exercise along with the rest of the soldiers. When coming home from exercise, my master was sure to be heard crying my name a quarter of a mile's distance from the house, at which I had to run out to meet him and carry his sword home. These, and other sufferings of the like nature, prepared me for my subsequent career, and fitted me for the journey on the desert. The circumstances which relieved me of my present master were as singular as the many unlooked-for whippings I received. One evening, when the sun was going down, and everything assuming the quietude of an eastern calm, a certain Arab came to our house, with whom I was desired to go and fetch some soap. I left everything behind me, and went on my supposed errand. Having arrived at the man's house, he asked my name, and told me that I was his property. I merely answered his reply by a look, for ere this time I had become quite regardless of my fate. My new master, whose name was Jubalee, was a native of Dongola, and had come to Kordofan on a trading excursion. He was in company with two others of the names of Auchmet and Mahomet from the same town. Mahomet, the youngest of the two, was a cruel monster, torturing and beating the slaves without any occasion. Auchmet was moderate. My master was of a quiet resigned temper, unless too much interfered with, and very seldom whipped any of his slaves. Having gathered six of us, they now thought of starting for their native country; and to this effect preparations were soon made. They procured four camels, a horse, and other necessaries for travelling, and started, shaping their course to the banks of the Nile. Travelling in these eastern countries is attended with many perilous situations, those engaged in it being exposed to starvation from want of water, liable to be attacked by beasts which have reliquished their first subordination, and entirely under the mercy of the monsoons.

* A strong wind which raises the sand, by which means many have been buried alive in the eastern deserts.

Our journey (before reaching the banks of the Nile) occupied ten days. Many were the privations we suffered on our way, sometimes from the excessive heat of the sun, and sometimes from want of water. During the middle of the day, we were so much overpowered by the heat, that we often had to delay our journey. At another time we had to exist a whole day without water, under the following circumstances: The water camel, of which I had a particular charge, was going before all the rest, and, unfortunately came, upon a dead camel lying on the road. The sight and smell of this animal soon spirit-stirred it, and the result was, that it danced and ran through thick and thin till the water bags, which were hanging on each side of the saddle, were destroyed, having come in contact with some wood on the side of the saddle. Fortune, however, had not altogether turned her face from us, for, in the evening, we came to some wells, where we supplied ourselves and rested for the night. From this place we pursued our journey to the banks of the Nile, and pitched our tents in the valley of Senaar, only a short distance from the town. My master left me here with the old man, two of the slaves, and a camel. Taking with him Mahomet, and the rest of the travelling appendages, he went to the town of Senaar, and there stayed for about a fortnight. During the whole of my time here, I had very little to occupy me, so I ran about through the different places without the least danger of meeting with a second kidnap. The vale at that time was in its prime, the trees having on their coats of variegated green; the grass, the herbs, and flowers, in full bloom; in short, everything was so beautiful, that nature seemed to contradict the wickedness of the world. Happening one day to go to the river side, I observed something uncommon moving on the water, with some white sheets filled with wind, as I thought. I had a dish in which I intended to have carried some water home, but on seeing this curious spectacle approaching me, I took to my heels, and leaving the dish behind, presented myself almost breathless before the old man. On explaining to him the appearance of the sight I had seen, he reprimanded my silliness, and told me that it was a ship, assuring me that it would injure no person, provided the people on board kept quiet, so I went back for my dish. This was the first time I ever saw a ship. My master arriving from Senaar soon after, we started, with an additional number of merchants from the town, and proceeded to Dongola. These merchants were not possessed of slaves, but had a great number of camels, and horses, and donkeys, thus making a formidable caravan. For three or four days we shaped our course along the banks of the Nile, under the direction of one of the native Arabs. At the end of that time, we prepared for a journey on the Libyan desert.

Our Arab guide now left us to pilot ourselves, and returned home. I was entirely deprived of a ride on any of the camels, being engaged in leading my old friend, the water camel, which was now turned into an hospital. One of the female slaves having grown ill with a mortal swelling in her thigh, could not walk, and, in consequence, I had to lead the camel on which she rode for nearly a month while crossing the desert. She grew worse and worse every day till she died, and was buried in the sand, without coffin or anything, while her death was not commemorated by the shedding of a single tear. Such are the horrors of the slave trade. Well do I remember the evening of her death. The sun was going down, the azure sky appeared to witness the end with calmness and composure, while the surrounding aspect threw a deep gloom over all our proceedings. I was thrown far behind the rest of the travellers; my fellow companion in slavery began to totter on her saddle, and death was soon announced by her falling from the camel. She was a native of Durfur,--a woman in the zenith of her life. The death of this unfortunate female put me in permanent possession of the camel during the remainder of the journey. By this time I became a great favourite with my master; and on one occasion he broke his walking cane over the back of one of the slaves on account of having taken the chief seat on my camel from me. Constrained by sorrow afterwards, my master desired me not to tell how his cane was broken. From the tediousness of our journey, we were glad to see Old Dongola, which predicted our nearness to the point of our destination. This town is situate on the banks of the Nile, and is distinguished for its ruins. We stayed here a short time to recruit our strength, and then proceeded to New Dongola, along the river's banks. A few days saw us home, and on our arrival, the different masters separated, each taking a share of the spoil with him. Auchmet, the eldest, took two of the slaves and a camel; Jubalee took for his share three of the slaves--one having died in the desert; and Mahomet took the rest of the live stock. I was only a few days with my master at his home when I was purchased by Mahomet's father. Mahomet's father and mother were two aged persons, and wished me to be a companion to them while their son followed his occupation. But their next door neighbour having expressed a desire for me to keep his shop, I was accordingly sold to him. I did not like my new master so well as the two former ones,--he often behaving cruelly to his slaves. I was generally very fortunate in keeping out of the many whippings which the rest received. On taking me to his house, he gave me some meat, and immediately after took me to his shop, about half a mile from the house. He was a dealer in all sorts of spices and gums,--the produce of the country. His shop was in one of the Dongola arcades, and was situated between a doctor's and a jeweller's. Besides myself, another young man, of the name of Salama, graced the shop door. Salama and I became great friends, and often went together to play by the water side. After the shop was shut one evening, we traced our steps, as usual, to the river's side, but what was my singular astonishment on perceiving a female at a distance whom I thought I knew. On going up to her, whom should I see but my old friend, Medina. Salama stood quite astonished when he heard her call me her brother. A small explanation, however, soon settled him. Medina took us to her master's house, and introduced us to her fellows, but our time being limited, we had to leave and get home as quick as possible, promising to return and see them again. This was a thing which we never accomplished while together, for Salama was sold soon after. A few days after this event, Salama and I happened to fall in with a pistol and some powder in the shop. Curiosity induced us to load it. Being the first time I had examined a pistol closely, I desired Salama to fire. He went to the window, and putting the mouth of it out to the open air, fired it off, and loaded it again, asking me to fire it off next. Instead of using the same precautions as he did, I fired it off in the shop, which caused a great smell of powder in the arcade. This induced the neighbours to investigate every place closely, who found that the greatest smell proceeded from our shop. They accordingly took hold of Salama, and would have thrashed him had he not put the blame upon me. I now took to my heels and ran for it, but my limbs were not sufficient to escape so many pursuers in the arcade; in consequence I was captured, and received such a thrashing as I did not forget in a very short time. Luckily our master was away from the shop at the time of this occurrence. Contrary to our expectations, he only gave a laugh when he was informed of our conduct. Soon after our master found out that it was not adequate to keep two of us in the shop, and accordingly sold my friend, Salama. I was now obliged to deal alone among the spices. I made out to pay another visit to Medina, who always gave me a kind reception, and had a little more time to relate our respective histories. I found that I was with my seventh master, whilst she was only with her fifth. Our time being so uncertain, we always bid each other good bye for ever, and it proved so on this occasion. Two or three days after, my master brought a man to the shop, who carefully scrutinized me after the manner of the slave traders, and then I was desired to follow him as my future owner.

Without taking farewell of my fellow slaves who were at the house, I was obliged to abandon everything and follow him. Hemet Hether (for that was the man's name) was a person of a pleasant countenance, a native of Berber, or as it is called by the inhabitants, Barbary. It is a small tract of country lying in the wilds of Upper Egypt, inhabited by a mild race of people, who addict themselves chiefly to agricultural interests. Hemet Hether took me by the hand and led me through the streets of Dongola to the suburbs of the town. We arrived at his brother's house, situate a few miles out of town, where two of his sons were waiting to receive us. I was put into a room where two other slaves were sitting, and with them I soon entered into conversation. The one was a boy the other a girl; the former from Durfur, the latter from Senaar. Our master was merely staying at his brother's for the purpose of gathering slaves, as his home was nearly a month's journey from Dongola, on the way to Cairo, a small village, called by the natives Goortie. Having gathered three of us, he and his sons now thought of going home, and began to prepare accordingly. We started on a morning when the sun was shining on the green fields of corn with bright illumination, and marched along till we found ourselves in a desert country. Before I left Dongola, my old master, Jubalee (having heard that a travelling merchant had bought me), came and gave my character as being an excellent traveller, and mentioned several incidents to ratify that belief on my present master's mind. For this reason I was entrusted with one of the camels. After going through the usual difficulties to be expected in the desert, we arrived at Goortie. The many congratulations which my master received on this occasion were indescribable. His wife kissing him, with tears of joy in her eyes, his daughter clinging to his neck, and the neighbours shaking hands with him, all showed friendship in the superlative degree.

Here I write this small poem:--

THO' LOST TO SIGHT, TO MEMORY DEAR.

How can the mother's loving eye
Part with the children whom she
bore;
Her sons are called, they'll not deny,
To serve on some far distant shore.
Swift time may soar on lofty wing,
With patience yet she'll stand and
bear;
She knows they're gone to serve
their king,
"Tho' lost to sight, to memory dear."

How can the loving husband's eye
Look from the wife he holds so
dear:
She soon his secrets does descry,
He tells them all without a fear.
But business calls him soon apart,
From her he holds so dear and near;
He near forgets her from his heart,
"Tho' lost to sight, to memory dear."

But who can mark the sacred glance,
Two lovers bear when doom'd to
part;
They part for months, for years,
perchance,
Far from those scenes which cheer
the heart.
They wait fair fortune's future day,
In hopes to meet some distant year;
Tho' parted far, true love can say,
"Tho' lost to sight, to memory dear."

Let such as court dear friendship's
path,
Pass happy days with friendship
here;
Let all forget the way to wrath,
In mutual love let all adhere.
Let those who cherish in their heart
The thoughts--"Tho' absent, ever
dear,"
Remember that although they part,
"Tho' lost to sight, to memory dear."

The time had not arrived when slave-dealers
went to Cairo to dispose of their slaves, in
consequence we had to stay at Goortie for three
months, during which time I was employed in doing
sundry things. First of all, I was sent to live with a
friend of my master's, who behaved very kindly to
me. Here I had to take care of some cows, while the

man's two sons attended to the lands of the farm, which were between three and four miles from the house. About six miles from Goortie, my master married a young woman, with whom I was soon taken to live. In many of the eastern countries, and particularly Egypt, a man is not confined to one wife, but can keep as many as his abilities will allow him. My master's recent marriage was the cause of raising a deal of jealousy on the part of the old one. He chiefly resided at the house he had built for the former, and when the latter met him they were sure to quarrel about something or other. On one occasion, being sent with some corn to the old lady's, on a donkey's back, she would not allow me to empty the sacks, so I had to stand for about half a day to await my master's arrival. On his coming up to me, he asked me why I did not empty the sacks? I told him my reason; after which he went into the house, and a quarrel ensued. The neighbours gathered about the house, and tried to prevent the quarrel; but, my master being in a passion, they found great difficulty in getting him quieted. After he had broken a great number of things, they managed to get him out of the house, and I obtained liberty to empty my sacks and return home. My master also returned to his new wife's, and never went back to Goortie, till within a few days of leaving for Cairo. The slave-ship landed in its season at Goortie, and took us on board. We arrived at the first cataracts of the Nile, and it being impracticable for the ship to proceed farther, we had to change our quarters. The masters busied themselves looking out for another ship to contain their menagerie of human beings. For this purpose we had to travel by land, and finally to sleep on land, before embarking again. Our new ship was a small one, and could not contain all our luggage without a crush; in consesequence, some of the slaves sickened, and were paid for their trouble by receiving a good flogging. After a fortnight had elapsed, we landed within a few miles of Cairo, in order to make ourselves look as fresh as daisies before entering the city. From this place we were made to march in military order. The grown up slaves led the van, and I, along with other young ones, marched in the rear, while our masters kept on the flanks. On reaching the entrance to the royal city, we were all counted by a man appointed for that purpose, who found that there were forty of us and ten masters. As soon as the counting was over, each master took his slaves and separated. Our master took us to an acquaintance of his, where he disposed of us, one after the other, but not before two months elapsed. We were regularly taken and exhibited in the slave market, where purchasers came to pick and choose. The grown up ones soon went off, while the small live stock remained for a long time in the market. A month after, my master shifted to another part of the town, a place near the barracks of Cairo. Here there were several of his countrymen, (under the employ of the Pacha,) whose duty it was to keep the gate of a manufactory of sundry wares. In this place he left me, and went away, but where I could not tell. A week or ten days after he returned for me, and took me to my old quarter, the slave market, where he soon disposed of

me. My ninth master was a European gentleman, of
the name of P----. With Mr. P---- I only lived a
fortnight, when I was dispatched (under charge of a
Turk) down to Alexandria. The next master into
whose hands I fell was R---- T----, Esq., British
Consul in Egypt. Having fallen into the hands of a
British gentleman, I now thought that I was lost,
having heard so many Mahommedan prejudices
against Christians. Contrary to my expectation,
however, I was treated with the greatest clemency,
received many indulgences which I never met with
before, and what completed my happiness was the
pains which Mr. L----, my master's son-in-law, took
in learning me to read and write. When he found it
impossible to teach me himself, the duty devolved
upon Mrs. S----, the housekeeper. I found much
gratification in this novel treatment, and expected to
know great things by it. Mrs. L., who took great
charge of me, never failed in seeing that I was
comfortable. While all the African formalities were
exchanging for European fashions, four months
elapsed, after which the family sailed up the Nile to
the first cataracts, taking me, and Mrs. S----, and an
Italian servant, of the name of Jacquomo. The first
cataracts are about 400 miles from Alexandria. A
whole month was spent in going and coming back
from the cataracts; and the objects which occupied
the particular attention of the family were the
ancient buildings then standing in ruins. On the left
bank of the Nile, and at some distance from Cairo,
the Egyptian pyramids present a huge spectacle,
having the appearance of small hills. These and
many other edifices were built in the distant ages of

antiquity, when the Egyptian monarchy flourished under its native dynasty. It is now a country ruled by a despotic viceroy. The native Egyptians are a quiet, inoffensive people, rather darker than the decendants of Ishmael, and still devote their time to learning, not seeming to have forgot the noble propensities of their ancestors. Architecture had been carried to its highest eminence by the Egyptians three thousand years before the Christian era. The ruins are scattered throughout the whole country. There are several old ruins at the cataracts, and these, along with the waterfalls, form the most romantic scenery imaginable. On our way home, the family visited Thebes and other places of antiquity. Arriving at Alexandria, my master, along with Mr. and Mrs. L., soon prepared for another journey. Taking Mr. and Mrs. S---- with them, they took the steamer to Malta. This was the first steam-boat I ever had been in, and was curious to know how the vessel went without sails. I asked one of the sailors, who explained the whole mystery by telling me that it went upon wheels. Five days and five nights on the Mediterranean brought us to Malta--a beautiful island, under the British Government. During our quarantine at Lazarett, my master sent Mr. and Mrs. S---- by a vessel bound for England, while we were confined for three weeks at this place previous to our entering the town. No foreigner is allowed to go to the town of Malta without riding quarantine for a certain length of time. Our time elapsing in this place of confinement, the family went to the town, stayed a short time there, and then set sail for Messina, in Sicily, but the sea grew so boisterous that the vessel (which was but a small one) had to return to Malta again. I had fallen asleep during the night, and was not aware of our return till morning. When I went on deck I learned that the family had gone ashore during the night, while the sailors, who were all Maltese, told me that they were desired to remunerate their toils by appropriating me to themselves. I began to cry, and and could not be pacified till they assured me to the contrary. They gave me some breakfast, and two of them (who had received previous instructions) took me to my master.

In a short time after, we again set out to Messina in a larger ship; and, after two days sail, arrived safe at the long-looked-for place. At Messina my master's nephew (Mr. H---- T----) awaited our arrival, and took us to his house. Here we stayed for sometime, and then went to Naples, where my master left Mr. and Mrs. L----, and proceeded to England. Having left Naples in the evening, the Italian steamer sailed the whole night; and next day, by twelve o'clock, landed us at Leghorn, and there we had to fork for our dinner on shore. Although we were taken on board upon condition of getting everything, they played us the same trick at two other places. When the vessel arrived at Genoa, my master betook himself to inland travelling, wishing to cross the continent, and sail over the channel to England. In pursuance of this scheme, he got a carriage from Genoa to Milan. In the suburbs of Milan my master was met by Mr. J--, another son-in-law. After staying a short time here, we left for England. Mr. J. also left his family and accompanied my master. We traversed the continent, and parmanently crossed the channel from Rotterdam to London.

Having entered Britain, I shall now celebrate the occasion by writing an ode to the country to which many of my countrymen owe their freedom, and liberty of conscience:--

ODE TO BRITAIN.

Surrounded by the foaming surge,
The Queen of land and sea;
For who can boast of Nelson's arms,
Or Wellington's, as thee.

Britain, thou land of peace and joy,
How strong thy bulwarks are;
Thou standest far above the world,
And that without a par.

All nations do thy seamen fear,
Thy ships they see with awe;
Allegiance, too, and homage pay,
As e'er fair Albion saw.

Thy vet'rans prove a fatal scourge,
To those who thee offend;

To those who court thy shelt'ring
arms,
Protection dost extend.
Thou wavest high the flag of fame,
Liberty is thy theme,
And while the exile seeks thy shore,
Salvation dost proclaim.

They hail thee as the stranger's
home,
The freedom of the slave;
Thy motto is--"Where'er I go,
"The captive I will save."

The ancient empires, what were
they,
When thus compared with thee?
The powers of Media, Greece, and
Rome,
Thy fame did never see.

ADDITIONAL POEMS.

THE SKY.

Methinks, when I the world behold,
What things this earth is made to
hold,
Creation has not spared her pains,

To show the powers of Him who
reigns.

The light blue and transparent sky,
Tells man his mind to lift on high,
And bids him view the ethereal
light,
"That beams upon his ravish'd
sight."

The sun, by day, with ardent mirth,
Glows on the cold unfeeling earth:
The moon and stars begin their
sway,
And shed their light till morning
day.

O look to that palacious view,
Which stands in colours red and
blue;
Resign thy fate submissively
To Him who lives above the sky.

No human fiends there can we fear;
No earthly foes above that sphere.
But He who reigns in yonder realm
Wields care's crown with a mercy's
helm.

BATTLE OF GWALIOR.

'Twas when the shades of ev'ning
fell
On India's lofty hills of snow:
That eve the minds will ne'er forget
Of those who have escap'd the blow.

'Twas on that eve that Gough did
say,
Prepare to fight whene'er you start,
For we will seize Gwalior's fort:
Maharajpoor shall know we're
smart.

As soon's the morn began to dawn
Each soldier stood with sword in
hand
Resolved to fight with all his might
Or die upon a foreign land.

In columns three they stood array'd
With all their force to face the foe;
From high Gwalior's fort look'd
down,
And threw her balls on them below.

Brave Thacwell stood, and at the

head
Of the first column did command,
Valiant, with grace, the second took,
While Dennis at the third did stand.

They fought with might and eager
true
For Britain's fame and Britain's
name,
Till they beheld Maharajpoor
Invested with a fire and flame.

The guns were then to silence
called,
Each man to charge with sword in
hand
With bay'nets fix'd they did
advance,
And shook Gwalior's fort and land.
Gwalior yielded power to them,
Maharajpoor a treaty sign'd,
The British march'd within their
bounds,
And left the conquer'd all behind.

ECLIPSE OF THE MOON.

Led by ambition's mighty force,
A friend and I did take our course

To view the eclipse upon the moon:
We wished to see ere late or soon.

We walked with slow and gentle
pace;
Perceived darkness on the moon's
trace.
Nought we saw but the cloudy sky;
Nought we heard but the Zephyr's
sigh.

All nature lay without alarms,
Wrapt silently in Morpheus' arms.
Nocturnal bliss had lull'd to rest
The chirps of the robin red breast.

While thus our thoughts did wander
o'er
Proud nature's wide creative power,
We saw as if reluctantly
The moon peep through the cloudy
sky.

Far through the azure of the sky
She stood downcast and ghastly shy.
One minute pass'd and she was gone
Behind her cloudy misty throne.

THE SEASONS.

In winter's freezing frost and wind
How sad the hills and mountains
stand,
While ice and snow do fill the
plains,
And seal the wide and mighty
strand.

The rivers look with mournful gaze;
The hills return their woeful song.
Why does the sun refuse to shine,
And leave us pedling in the throng?

Up starts nature and exclaims,
Why do ye look so sour and sad?
The sun will come and bring again
With him the warm luxuriant plaid.

The voice of spring is heard afar
Proclaim the sun and summer nigh,
While all the birds do sing with joy,
And soar with grace along the sky.

The trees begin to flourish green;
The flowers appear above the
ground;

The sun shines with glittering rays,
Diffusing mirth to all around.

Clad with a light translucent robe,
The God of summer glides along.
His "cheering" breath and
"glad'ning" rays
Give life and health to weak and
strong.

See how the stream glides in the
vale
To join the sea with rapid pace.
The fruit begins to ripen fast;
The flowers bloom with lovely
grace.
But hark! who comes with sheaf of
corn
Wrapt round her head with grapes
so fine?
Ah! 'tis Pomona in her prime,
Godess of harvest and the vine.

The winter comes, when she
departs;
The spring it bids the birds to sing;
While summer days with mirth
return,
Autumnus tries the fruit to bring.

Incidents Connected with the Life of Selim Aga